T0209291

Healing
EMOTIONAL WOUNDS

THIRTY-DAY
JOURNAL

TOSHA MCRANEY

WESTBOW
PRESS®
A DIVISION OF THOMAS NELSON
& ZONDERVAN

WestBow Press books may be ordered through booksellers or by contacting:

WestBow Press
A Division of Thomas Nelson & Zondervan
1663 Liberty Drive
Bloomington, IN 47403
www.westbowpress.com
844-714-3454

Because of the dynamic nature of the Internet, any web addresses or links contained in this book may have changed since publication and may no longer be valid. The views expressed in this work are solely those of the author and do not necessarily reflect the views of the publisher, and the publisher hereby disclaims any responsibility for them.

Any people depicted in stock imagery provided by Getty Images are models, and such images are being used for illustrative purposes only. Certain stock imagery © Getty Images.

Scripture quotations marked KJV are taken from the King James Version.

Scripture quotations marked NKJV are taken from the New King James Version®. Copyright © 1982 by Thomas Nelson. Used by permission. All rights reserved.

Scripture quotations marked ESV taken from The Holy Bible, English Standard Version® (ESV®), Copyright © 2001 by Crossway, a publishing ministry of Good News Publishers. All rights reserved.

Scripture quotations marked NLT are taken from the Holy Bible, New Living Translation, Copyright © 1996, 2004, 2015 by Tyndale House Foundation. Used by permission of Tyndale House Publishers, Inc., Carol Stream, Illinois 60188. All rights reserved.

ISBN: 978-1-6642-8930-7 (sc)
ISBN: 978-1-6642-8931-4 (hc)
ISBN: 978-1-6642-8929-1 (e)

Print information available on the last page.

WestBow Press rev. date: 01/18/2023

DEDICATION

First, I would like to thank my Lord, Jesus. Thank you for saving and healing me. I have released this word to your people, and I ask you to anoint it and send it to every heart who needs to hear it. I am also so thankful for my pastor and his wife, Jerry and Ruth Terrell, for pouring wisdom into me throughout the years. To my parents, Hazel and Chuck, thank you for the life and love you've given me. To my husband, Mark, and my four girls, Stacey, Chloe, Bailey, and Brooklyn, a million thank-yous for all the time that you've allowed me to spend serving the Lord, teaching my classes, and writing this book. Girls, I am grateful to be your mom. A shout-out to the ladies at the Refuge for all their support in writing this book. And a personal thank-you from the bottom of my heart to Lileana Ríos-Ledezma, for walking me through the very last mile of editing this book. I love you all.

"So Jesus answered and said, "Assuredly, I say to you, there is no one who has left house or brothers or sisters or father or mother or wife or children or lands, for My sake and the gospel's, who shall not receive a hundredfold now in this time—houses and brothers and sisters and mothers and children and lands, with persecutions—and in the age to come, eternal life" (Mark 10:29–30, NKJV).

CONTENTS

CONTENTS

DAY 1

REJECTION AND STRONGHOLDS

According to *Merriam-Webster*, the definition of *rejection* is to feel refused, not accepted, or dismissed. This wound can make us feel unwanted and cause feelings of being unloved or not good enough. When a person feels rejected and subsequently unwanted, it can also cause he or she to lash out in many unhealthy ways.

Healing

"When my father and mother forsake me, then the Lord will take me up" (Psalm 27:10, KJV).

The Word tells us that even if our parents reject us, the Lord will pick us up and hold us close. It almost seems as if the more we are abandoned, the closer God draws us to Him. He will be our parent, spouse, and friend. "The Lord has appeared to me of old, saying, 'Yea I have loved you with an everlasting love therefore with lovingkindness I have drawn thee'" (Jeremiah 31:3 KJV). Remember, He loves us with an everlasting love that doesn't end. He accepts us and draws us near with love and kindness. He isn't a big, mean, angry God.

Reflection Journal

What are some things that have caused you to feel rejected and unwanted in your life? Examples: being a child battled over in a divorce, work hurts, bad relationships, unhealthy friendships, church hurts, or family hurts.

_____

_____

_____

_____

_____

How did you lash out or act in that season of your life? Examples: in anger, depression, rage, or outbursts; by building walls or shutting down; or by people pleasing.

_____

_____

_____

_____

_____

Now that you know feeling rejected can cause these negative feelings and reactions, remind yourself often with songs and scriptures that you are loved and wanted. No human, substance, or possession is big enough to fill and heal us. The only things that can heal the wounds of rejection are God's never-ending love and His Word.

Suggested Songs to Listen to Today or When You Are Dealing with Rejection

- Dara Maclean's "You Are Wanted"
- Olivia Lane's "Woman at the Well"
- Lauren Daigle's "You Say"

DAY 2

LONELINESS

This wound often starts as a child and follows us into adulthood. It includes the absence of parents or people we cared about being absent when we needed them the most. Even as adults, our needs and desires are often overlooked and neglected. After a person has suffered from loneliness, it can cause a dark cloud to appear even in times when we shouldn't feel lonely anymore. We must learn to speak to the sad, dark cloud that tries to creep back in and to tell it that it has no place in our life anymore. We are not that child or person anymore, and it must leave. Also, we must remember loneliness isn't just the absence of people. It's the absence of purpose, and when we feel lonely, we can use our time to search God for our purpose in this world because He never leaves us. We are not alone, and we never will be. We may not have known to talk to Him and seek Him, but now we do.

Healing

"Where can I go from Your Spirit? Or where can I flee from Your presence? If I ascend into heaven, You are there; If I make my bed in hell, behold, You are there. If I take the wings of the morning, and dwell in the uttermost parts of the sea, Even there Your hand shall lead me, and Your right hand shall hold me" (Psalm 139:7–10, NKJV).

"Be strong and of good courage, do not fear nor be afraid of them; for the LORD your God, He is the One who goes with you. He will not leave you nor forsake you." (Deuteronomy 31:6, NKJV).

Reflection Journal

At what times in your life do you remember feeling lonely?

_____

_____

_____

_____

_____

Now that you know God is always with you to talk to and to seek His purpose, will you seek Him? If so, what are a few things you have thought that God may want to use you to do? Write them down. Examples: sing, pray for people, teach, preach, work with the brokenhearted, help young or old people, or write a book.

_____

_____

_____

_____

_____

Remember that you can speak to that sad, dark cloud, tell it to leave, and remind it that you are not that old person anymore. I'm not that little girl I used to be!

"For assuredly, I say to you, whoever says to this mountain, 'Be removed and be cast into the sea,' and does not doubt in his heart, but believes that those things he says will be done, he will have whatever he says. Therefore, I say to you, whatever things you ask when you pray, believe that you receive them, and you will have them" (Mark 11:23–24, NKJV).

DAY 3

HARSH WORDS

Some of us have grown up with people who have sharp tongues full of harsh words. Having sharp and harsh words thrown at a tender mind causes damage. It may not be seen with the naked eye, but the wounds are real nonetheless.

Healing

"A soft answer turneth away wrath: but grievous words stir up anger" (Proverbs 15:1, KJV).

"There is one who speaks like the piercings of a sword, But the tongue of the wise promotes health" (Proverb 12:18, NKJV).

Harsh words pierce the soul like a sword, and grievous words stir up anger. Anger can cause an argument quickly. Unfortunately, a person spoken harshly to in the past often later becomes an angry person who speaks harshly to others.

Reflection Journal

When you were young or in any past relationship, were you spoken to harshly? If so, how did this affect your emotions, and did your personality change from the abuse?

_____

_____

_____

The wisdom of thinking before we speak and using gentle words instead of putting stingers on them turns away anger and heals wounds.

DAY 4

UNGODLY SOUL TIE

A soul tie is an emotional or physical pull to be with someone. People can be addicted to one another. Think about that: when we are dealing with an ungodly soul tie, it can cause us to feel pulled toward or attracted to someone who is bad for us and who will possibly cause a spiritual or physical death if we don't break that tie.

Healing
"Be not unequally yoked together with unbelievers: for what fellowship hath righteousness with unrighteousness? And what communion has light with darkness?" (2 Corinthians 6:14, KJV).

The Bible gives the example of not being yoked to an unbeliever. When animals were teamed together, they had to be able to go the same direction. A wooden instrument (yoke) was placed around their necks so they would go in the same direction and stay together. If two people who are teamed together desire to go different ways, one will drag the other along, miserably, or they will fight to the death. Do either of these sound like the life God has intended? This is why we do not want to be yoked to someone who is not going in the direction God has for us.

"He who walks with wise men will be wise, but the companion of fools will be destroyed" (Proverb 13:20, NKJV).

Reflection Journal

List people in your life you need to ask God if they are ungodly soul ties. Remember this can be a friendship or relationship.

_____

_____

_____

_____

_____

Breaking Free

1. Admit that you have an ungodly soul tie.
2. Ask God to forgive you for entering this friendship/relationship. Tell the Lord that you will break from this relationship and ask Him to deliver you from it.
3. Look at the person's life over the past five years and ask yourself if you would sign up to repeat another five years with that person. Would it be signing up for peace or torment?
4. Fasting can break anything that is not supposed to be in your life. Fast and ask God to do what you cannot do yourself. Fasting is going without food or only eating certain foods for a specific amount of time. During this time, you are praying and asking God to do for you supernaturally what you cannot do for yourself. An example of a fast could be three days of eating only fruits, vegetables, nuts, and water.
5. Finally, break all contact if possible. If not, set up boundaries and never be alone with this person again.

DAY 5

DEPRESSION

Depression often feels dark, negative, discouraging, and fearful. It causes us to doubt our self-worth and often question if we should exist or if we can do anything right. The longer we battle this, the harder it can be to get out of it. But God always has a plan. It is easier to stay out of depression than it is to pull ourselves out once we fall into it. Use the steps listed below to pull yourself out and keep yourself out of depression for good!

Healing

"And it came to pass, when the evil spirit from God was upon Saul, that David took a harp, and played with his hand: so Saul was refreshed, and was well, and the evil spirit departed from him" (1 Samuel 16:23, KJV).

1. Get up early and stay out of darkness. Darkness is a friend of depression. No matter what time you like to sleep until, be sure to push yourself to get up at least a little earlier.

2. Play Christian music around you. This will shift the atmosphere and push back the darkness that has come over you like a cloud. At first, you may have to play two positive songs to push back the depression enough to sit up in your bed. You may have to play two more positive songs to crawl out of bed. That's OK. Keep doing it, and you will win the fight.

3. Write ten positive things about yourself or about a situation that plagues you the most.

4. Read and write three scriptures on the four subjects that have been the biggest battles in your life. I always write the lies I hear on one side and the truth in God's Word on the other. Examples include marriage, feeling unwanted, suicide, discouragement, fear, or abuse. Remember, there are scriptures for every subject, and reading them breaks the enemy's power over you.

"Fear not, for I am with you; Be not dismayed, for I am your God. I will strengthen you, yes, I will help you, I will uphold you with My righteous right hand" (Isaiah 41:10, NKJV).

"I will praise You, for I am fearfully and wonderfully made; Marvelous are Your works, and that my soul knows very well" (Psalm 139:14, NKJV).

Reflection Journal

Lies
What are some of the negative lies you have heard about yourself in your head or from others?

_____

_____

_____

_____

_____

Truth
Write the truth from God's Word about each of the negative lies the enemy whispers about you or others.

_____

_____

TOSHA MCRANEY

_____

_____

_____

List a few songs you could play to speak the truth and to bring a positive atmosphere around your life. This will help chase away the darkness. It will stop the negative lies the enemy has been whispering to take you and your family out.

Listen to the song "Hello, My Name Is" by Mathew West.

While listening to this song, God revealed to me that some mornings, when I opened my eyes and felt the most depressing feeling that the spirit of defeat was at the foot of my bed throwing words at me like "You're ignorant," "Remember what you did," "Just go back to bed," or "You're unworthy," I would hear this and worse. Often, I would agree with it, put the pillow over my head, and go back to sleep to hide, but then I followed the steps I shared with you, and I don't have to do that ever again!

DAY 6

DIVISION

To divide is to separate something into parts. It is also, a disagreement between two people or groups typically causes tension or hostility. The enemy knows if he can cause us to divide, divorce, or separate from the things, people, or places our purposes are attached to, he can "divide and conquer us."

Healing

There are five steps you should go over before you divide or divorce from anything:

1. Ask God.

If I leave this person or place, will God go with me? David asked God in 1 Samuel 30, "If I go will you go with me?" God said yes, and David recovered everything he lost and was blessed.

2. Obey God.

Do things God's way and not our own. Even when it would seem better to do it our way. In 2 Samuel 13, Saul did things his way instead of God's way and he and his children died.

3. Make a list.

Make a list of ten good things about this person, place, or thing. Look at the positive closely before you listen to all the negatives being thrown into your mind.

4. Seek Godly counsel.

Before you make a life move, counsel with someone who is faithful to God and shows wisdom in their own life. Sometimes they can see over the mountain we are still climbing. "Without counsel purposes are disappointed: but in the multitude of counselors, they are established" (Proverb 15:22, KJV).

5. Wait.

Waiting can be so hard. I often say that waiting is a Christian curse word. No one wants to do it. We mostly ask what God wants us to do, but then we do what we've already decided to do. It's important to wait for his will to be revealed. "Wait on the LORD: be of good courage, and he shall strengthen thine heart: wait, I say, on the LORD" (Psalm 27:14, KJV).

Before we make any decisions to leave a person, place, or thing, let us say, "God, if I go, are you going with me?" and listen for his will.

Reflection Journal

Is there something the enemy often uses or sets up hostility with to tempt you to divide or leave it? If so, what, where, or who?

_____

_____

_____

_____

_____

DAY 7

CHOICES AND DECISIONS

To change our habits of making bad choices, we must admit that we have made bad choices in the past and, at times, we have looked into our own minds for answers instead of seeking God's will and obeying what he leads us to do.

Healing
"Trust in the LORD with all thine heart; and lean not unto thine own understanding. In all thy ways acknowledge him, and he shall direct thy paths" (Proverbs 3:5–6, KJV).

We must learn a healthy way to make choices and decisions in the future. There is a three-step pattern found in the word of God:

1. Trust God.
We must trust God. Do we trust Him to help us make decisions and do we ask him to show us what to do before we do it?

2. Lean not to our own understanding.
Confusion will stay in our minds if we continue to search our brain for the answers to life. The lord once showed me "you don't have the answers to life inside yourself. "I was driving myself senseless looking for answers only God has.

3. Acknowledge God, and he will direct you.
God will help us only in the areas we invite him into. It's simple: if we invite him into the process of a choice or decision, then he will help. He

will not force his way in if we do not invite him. "Acknowledge God, and he will direct you" means that if we ask him about what to do, he will tell us. Remember, this scripture we can see comes with a promise. He promised that if we trust him enough to acknowledge him, then he will direct us on the ways to go and not to go. Lord, helps us always to acknowledge you before we make choices and decisions on our own.

Reflection Journal

Can you admit you have made some bad choices and decisions in your past? List a few.

_____

_____

_____

_____

_____

List something you need to decide on and need God's direction. Writing it will acknowledge him so he can start to direct you.

_____

_____

_____

_____

_____

DAY 8

WHAT ABOUT ME?

One of the hardest seasons of life is when a person goes through deep feelings of "what about me?" I've heard this called the curse of Esau. When Esau realized that his brother, Jacob, had received his blessing instead him, he asked, "Is nothing left for me, father?" Have you had a situation where someone else got what you prayed for, stole something from you, left you all alone when you needed them most, or been in any situation that made you feel completely betrayed, alone, or forgotten? We all have, but there is healing from this potentially fatal spiritual wound.

Healing

To be healed from this deep wound, we will have to do a deep study on God's character. God is a God who loves us. A God who loves us will not allow these things unless a miraculous purpose will be born on the other side. Remind yourself of these two things:

1. He can turn the bad into good and bless you even more in due time.

Jacob stole Esau's birthright, but when they met fourteen years later, Esau refused Jacob's gifts because he was so rich, and he didn't need them. He had four hundred men with him. This shows you how he had prospered. Jacob had been blessed but had also been a slave for the last fourteen years. God knows how to work out things that were bad. He also knows how to turn them for your good—in due season. Read Genesis 32:6.

"But as for you, you meant evil against me; but God meant it for good, in order to bring it about as it is this day, to save many people alive" (Genesis 50:20, NKJV).

"And we know that all things work together for good to them that love God, to them who are the called according to his purpose" (Romans 8:28, KJV).

"And let us not be weary in well doing for in due season we shall reap if we faint not" (Galatians 6:9, KJV).

2. You are wanted and loved by God.
When you're questioning "what about me," you must do a study on being loved and wanted by God. He chose us before he built the world.

"Just as He chose us in Him before the foundation of the world, that we should be holy and without blame before Him in love" (Ephesians 1:6, NKJV).

He knew you and spent time with you before you were born. So surely, he didn't miss what just happened in your life, and he is busy making it all turn to good.

"Before I formed thee in the belly, I knew thee; and before thou camest forth out of the womb I sanctified thee, and I ordained thee a prophet unto the nations" (Jeremiah 1:5, KJV).

He loves you eternally, and his love is everlasting. You're not alone; he didn't leave you, and he is strong enough to carry you through this season if you will let him.

"The LORD has appeared of old to me, saying: 'Yes, I have loved you with an everlasting love; Therefore, with lovingkindness I have drawn you'" (Jeremiah 31:3, NKJV).

Reflection Journal

What season are you going through or have you recently been through that left you feeling all alone or saying, "What about me?"

_____

_____

_____

_____

_____

DAY 9

LIBERTY AND DELIVERANCE

Most of us have struggled to cover emotional pains, struggled with addictions, or had a sin take control in our lives. If we look back, most things we use for comfort are fun in the beginning, but later, we realize we are bound to them and that they no longer feel like a choice. We have lost our liberty or our freedom. How do we get it back? Where can we find deliverance?

Healing

So, after we have lost our liberty (freedom) how do we get it back? The word of God tells us that Wherever the Spirit of the Lord is that there is liberty there.

"Now the Lord is that Spirit: and where the Spirit of the Lord is, there is liberty" (2 Corinthians 3:17, KJV).

Where is the Spirit of the Lord, so I can go these places and find my liberty?

1. Talking to God.
When you pray, you talk to God, and he is there.

2. His Word.
When you pick up God's Word and begin to read or listen to it, you enter into his presence, and he talks to you.

3. Going to church or classes where his Spirit is.

There is a part of deliverance that comes only from the power of God. You will know when you enter a place of learning and worship, and God's presence and power are there. Go to these places often to get free and to stay free. If you do not feel God's presence and power in your place of worship, ask God to lead you to one where you do. "And my speech and my preaching was not with enticing words of man's wisdom, but in demonstration of the Spirit and of power" (1 Corinthians 2:4, KJV).

4. Godly music.

Listening to godly music not only brings his presence and freedom but darkness will also flee. "And it came to pass, when the evil spirit from God was upon Saul, that David took a harp, and played with his hand: so, Saul was refreshed, and was well, and the evil spirit departed from him" (1 Samuel 16:23, KJV).

Once you get your liberty and deliverance, remember everything it takes to get free and to stay free.

"Stand fast therefore in the liberty wherewith Christ hath made us free and be not entangled again with the yoke of bondage" (Galatians 5:1, KJV).

Reflection Journal

List three things you are struggling with or that you are chained to and from which you need God's help finding liberty and deliverance. For example: drugs, gambling, unhealthy food, lust, pornography, negative attention, prescription medications, or alcohol.

_____

_____

_____

_____

_____

When was the last time you went to a place of worship where you could feel the power of God? When is the next time you can attend?

_____

_____

_____

_____

_____

STUCK IN THE PAST

Many of us think constantly of pain, losses, and failures from our pasts. I want you to think of these bad memories as tombs—things that should be looked at and learned from and then buried. There is a story in Mark 5 about a man who the Bible calls insane. It says that he was in the tombs day and night, cutting himself. Many of us mentally and emotionally cut ourselves off by dwelling among the tombs of our past issues that we have refused to let go of. Or sometimes we worry day and night about future things that are beyond our control. Read Mark 5: "And always, night and day, he was in the mountains, and in the tombs, crying, and cutting himself with stones" (Mark 5:5, KJV).

Healing
There are three steps to break these habits:

1. Recognize when your thoughts are on past pain, loss, failure, or future things beyond your control.

2. Stop worrying or fretting.
One definition of fretting is to "gnaw on like a bone." Remember, to fret is to worry about something over and over. When we do this, it can open a door for a spirit of depression, grief, or even insanity. "Fret not thyself ..." (Psalm 37:1, KJV).

3. Trust God to work things out for our good, even when they are currently not going great. "Trust in the LORD with all thine heart; and lean not unto thine own understanding. In all thy ways acknowledge him, and he shall direct thy paths." Proverbs 3:5–6 (KJV)

When we trust God, we acknowledge him with the pain, losses, or failures of our pasts, and we trust him to direct us, help us, and heal us. Look at the issue, learn from it, and bury it in the heart and hands of Jesus. He is trustworthy to heal it, help us, and one day work it out for our good.

Reflection Journal

Do you have pain, losses, or failures from your past that you think about often and can't seem to let go of? If so, list them.

_____

_____

_____

_____

_____

DAY 11

CHANGE

To change is to become different. Unfortunately, change usually causes pain before it brings blessings. In the world we live in, we like "microwave blessings." We like things done fast and with little effort on our parts. When a person actually succeeds at change, it's because the fear of staying the same has gotten stronger than the fear of how much a change will hurt. Our hearts can be lazy, and they can lie to us to make it OK to stay the same.

Healing
Three steps to successful change:

1. Knowledge.
It is important that we know what the word of God says about each subject in our lives. To do this, look up scriptures on the things you need to change. At times, we can't even change when our spouses, parents, kids, or even we want to. However, when we actually see how God feels about change, we are often motivated to do so.

2. Stop giving into your feelings and emotions.
The Bible teaches us that our hearts are deceitful and will lie to us. This is why we need to know how God feels about things and remind ourselves often that our feelings and desires may be lying to us. Just because it hurts, doesn't mean it's time to give up or give in.

"The heart is deceitful above all things, and desperately wicked: who can know it?" (Jeremiah 17:9, KJV).

3. Start putting your goals for change into action.

Change can be talked about for years. You have to reach out and make a physical move toward your goals. Call someone, join the gym, call a rehab center, sign up for those classes, or even admit your plans to a counselor or friend who will hold you accountable. Each time we don't change, we lose something else. Let's move forward today and begin our journeys to real change.

Reflection Journal

What is it going to take for you to change? If you don't change this time, what could you lose next? Is it worth it?

_____

_____

_____

_____

_____

What things in your life have you been wanting to change but haven't been able to push past the pain to do them?

_____

_____

_____

_____

_____

What can you do today to start the process of change in your life?

_____

_____

_____

_____

_____

DAY 12

DISCOURAGEMENT AND DEFEAT

When we get discouraged, it is the opposite of having courage. This is an important tool for the enemy. Everything we once thought of with hope, passion, and vision is replaced with a feeling of defeat. I've heard it said that discouragement is like putting rocks in your own backpack. It makes everything we do heavier and require more effort. This can happen to us very fast, and often we don't know where it came from. Symptoms are not having a desire to move forward or continue with a project, no desire to read or pray, low energy, and, at times, no desire to even attend the house of God. This is also known as a dry season.

Healing
Steps to overcoming being discouraged or defeated:

1. Listen to godly music to create an atmosphere of hope and courage around you.

2. Remind yourself how far God has brought you.
"And David was greatly distressed; for the people spake of stoning him, because the soul of all the people was grieved, every man for his sons and for his daughters: but David encouraged himself in the LORD his God" (1 Samuel 30:6, KJV).

3. Talk to someone who is encouraging.
As you talk to this person about how you are doing, the reason for the discouragement and defeat will usually identify itself. After we give up the negative feelings or thing, our joy will usually return.

4. Keep doing what you know to do, even when you don't feel like it.
As fast as the discouragement came, it can also leave. "When He works
on the left hand, I cannot behold Him; When He turns to the right
hand, I cannot see Him. But He knoweth the way that I take: when
He hath tried me, I shall come forth as gold" (Job 23: 9–10, NKJV).

Reflection Journal

Have you been discouraged lately or felt defeated about a situation?

_____

_____

_____

_____

Write down two miracles he has already done for you or for your family
in the past.

_____

_____

Who can you visit or call for positive godly counsel?

_____

_____

_____

_____

TOSHA MCRANEY

Remember that when the enemy tries to defeat you by reminding you of something discouraging, you can remind him that he was defeated when God punished him, cursed him, and took his legs.

"And the LORD God said unto the serpent because thou hast done this, thou art cursed above all cattle, and above every beast of the field; upon thy belly shalt thou go, and dust shalt thou eat all the days of thy life" (Genesis 3:14, KJV).

DAY 13

GUILT AND SHAME

It is impossible in this life to never do something that will cause us to feel guilt and shame. The most important thing is to learn how to deal with guilt without allowing it to cause shame and, in the end, cause us to give up. I had to learn that even if I gave up on myself, God would not give up on me until he has finished his work for me.

Healing
"And I am sure of this, that he who began a good work in you will bring it to completion on the day of Jesus Christ" (Philippians 1:6, ESV).

1. Admit that no one is perfect, including myself.
"For all have sinned, and come short of the glory of God" (Romans 3:23, NKJV).

2. Repent.
When we sin or mess up, there is already a plan set in place for our forgiveness. We must ask God to forgive our mistakes. After we do this, we must believe his word that he cleanses us even if we do not feel cleansed at first. Sometimes we have to stand on his promise that we are forgiven.

"If we confess our sins, He is faithful and just to forgive us our sins, and to cleanse us from all unrighteousness" (1 John 1:9, KJV).

3. Forgive.

We must forgive ourselves and others. The Bible is very specific: without forgiveness, no one will enter heaven. We must include forgiving ourselves in this list.

"Come now, and let us reason together," says the LORD, "Though your sins are like scarlet, they shall be as white as snow; Though they are red like crimson, they shall be as wool" (Isaiah 1:18, NKJV).

Reflection Journal

Is there something in your life that you need to admit, repent of, and forgive yourself for?

_____

_____

_____

_____

What is your favorite scripture in this lesson?

_____

_____

_____

_____

DAY 14

ENDURE

To endure is to suffer something painful or difficult and last or remain to the end. Everyone in life will suffer at some point. As Christians, God asks us to endure these painful situations or seasons and not to give up. He not only asks us to do this, but he himself was an example of suffering and endurance. Below are four examples of how we are asked to endure and are shown the way.

Healing

1. Jesus himself showed endurance and held on when he could have given up.

"For to this you were called, because Christ also suffered for us, leaving us an example, that you should follow His steps" (1 Peter 2:21, NKJV).

2. The God of the universe did not even make threats when being mistreated.

"Who, when He was reviled, reviled not again; when he suffered, he threatened not; but committed himself to him that judgeth righteously?" (1 Peter 2:23, NKJV).

3. Paul tells us many things he has suffered and has gained strength from being weak.

"For the sake of Christ, then, I am content with weaknesses, insults, hardships, persecutions, and calamities. For when I am weak, then I am strong" (2 Corinthians 12:10, ESV) .

4. One of the most encouraging scriptures on endurance.
Paul calls us out as soldiers for Christ to endure hardship as a good soldier. No matter what we are going through when we read this, we square our shoulders back and feel the courage to rise up to endure and carry our cross a little longer.

"You therefore must endure hardship as a good soldier of Jesus Christ" (2 Timothy 2:3, NJKV).

Reflection Journal

Have you endured some hardships like the disciples when, only for God's glory, were you able to endure like a good soldier of Christ and not give up?

_____

_____

_____

_____

What has been the hardest trial to endure as a Christian?

_____

_____

_____

_____

_____

STORMS

We have all had seasons in our lives where everything seemed to be going the wrong way. On the spiritual side, we call this a storm. There are four reasons a storm may have entered our lives.

Healing

1. Wake Up.
A storm can often be allowed into our lives to wake us up if we are headed in the wrong direction. At times, God really will allow us to have a wake-up call and an opportunity to turn around.

2. Wash Us.
Storms can be used to wash away some bad things we have picked up. He may see that we need to let go of them, and storms really do wash things off and make directions clearer after the dust is settled.

3. Miracles.
Often, a storm comes in the form of a huge problem that seems unfixable. God may use these things to bring forth his miracles and to show us that he is able to do the impossible.

4. Elevate.
Many times, storms are used to elevate us to the next level with God. The wind and pressure will check us for the ability to handle the next level, and when the sky clears, if we don't quit, we may find we have been elevated spiritually to the next level.

Reflection Journal

Have you been through a storm?

_____

_____

_____

_____

_____

_____

What reason do you think the storm may have come into your life?

_____

_____

_____

_____

_____

_____

What blessings did you receive on the other side of the storm?

_____

_____

_____

_____

_____

_____

"But may the God of all grace, who called us to His eternal glory by Christ Jesus, after you have suffered a while, perfect, establish, strengthen, and settle you" (1 Peter 5:10, KJV).

"Now no chastening for the present seemeth to be joyous, but grievous: nevertheless afterward it yieldeth the peaceable fruit of righteousness unto them which are exercised thereby" (Hebrew 12:11, KJV).

DAY 16

YOU ARE LOVED

Many of us struggle with feeling unloved, unwanted, lonely, and not really knowing who we are. God is in love with us, and he went before our first memories—and even before the world was created—to love us and give us a purpose.

Healing

"Just as He chose us in Him before the foundation of the world, that we should be holy and without blame before Him in love" (Ephesians 1:4, NKJV).

He chose us to be with him in love, before the foundation of the world was even formed. That is real love, a God who is in love with his children. No longer are we slaves to a master but sons and daughters to a heavenly Father who loves us. We were chosen before earth was built. Think about that. Loneliness is not just the absence of people, it's often the absence of purpose.

"Before I formed you in the womb, I knew you; Before you were born, I sanctified you; I ordained you a prophet to the nations" (Jeremiah 1:5, KJV).

Me? Before you formed me, you spent time with me, Lord? I read that you appointed Jeremiah to be a prophet. What did you appoint me to be? Did you know that God spent time with us and appointed each of us, in our mother's wombs, to be something? Have you ever asked him what it was? Over the next few weeks, ask him each day to reveal your purpose and point you in the direction he would have you go.

Reflection Journal

Have you struggled with feeling unloved, unwanted, and not knowing who you are supposed to be? If so, explain how you felt.

_____

_____

_____

_____

_____

Ask God, what is my purpose? What did you appoint me to be or do while I am on this earth?

_____

_____

_____

_____

_____

The LORD has appeared of old to me, saying: "Yes, I have loved you with an everlasting love; Therefore, with lovingkindness I have drawn you" (Jeremiah 31:3, NKJV).

God's love never ends. He loves us when we are mean, naughty, sad, ignoring him, and even when we are fighting against him. How many times did he protect us, forgive us, and draw us in with kindness? Even when we turn to the world and it chews us up and spits us out, we can hear a whispered, "Let me put you back together, my child." So many times, people hurt us or we hurt ourselves, and immediately he sets up opportunities for help, for healing, and for putting us back together, just as a good parent would. Also, remember that God loves us. He is not mad at us.

Listen to "Come as You Are" by Pocket Full of Rocks. The following words are part of the lyrics: "He is not mad at you. He is not disappointed. Bring him all your broken pieces and all your shameful scars. The pain you feel in your heart, bring it all to Jesus You can come as you are."

Additionally, listen to the song "Wanted" by Dara Maclean.

THE FAMILY WOUND

A family member or parent wound is something many people never overcome. Many people have something in their families or childhoods that left an emotional scar. Some will stay stuck in sadness and depression because of the things they never were able to get over; others may hide the pain behind anger, pride, addiction, denial, and many other things. One day, if we become parents, we will need mercy for our own failures. Today, let's get some healing from all that we went through. God asks us to honor our parents. Life has made that very hard for many of us. Even if they are way less than what we thought they should be, there is healing and power in mercy and forgiveness.

Healing

1. Admit and repent.
Admit to yourself and to God that you were hurt or offended, even if it was years ago. Writing the offense in detail helps bring it to the surface so we can prepare our heart to forgive. Ask God to forgive us for any part we had in the offense or failure of the relationship.

2. Forgive.
To forgive is to release a debt. To move forward, we must forgive the past. Ask God to forgive the person or people for their shortcomings. It often helps us forgive a family member or parent when we look at his or her childhood or current life and see what the person went through that may have caused him or her to be who that person is now.

3. Honor.

The Bible says to honor our fathers and mothers. What does that mean and how? To honor is to show respect. Sometimes the best honor we can have for our parents is by honoring them with mercy (undeserved forgiveness) or by not publicly slandering them for their mistakes. For example, Noah's son Ham, saw his father had passed from drinking too much and that he was naked in his tent. He went and told everyone and dishonored his father. Shem and Japheth, the other two sons of Noah, walked backward with a blanket and covered their father so no one else would see him; that is honor. Our parents were not always right, but we honor them by having mercy and by not publicly blasting them for their failures. Now, if your past with your parents contained sexual or physical abuse, then you needed to tell someone. As an adolescent or an adult, counseling may be needed for some of the things we went through, and that is never dishonoring. If we are blessed in the land for honor, then we are cursed in the land for dishonor. Ham's children were cursed for his dishonor. The Lord helps us find a way back to honor, so our children do not suffer. "Honor your father and your mother, that your days may be long upon the land which the LORD your God is giving you" (Exodus 20:12, NKJV).

4. Bless.

When we bless someone who has hurt us, we enter an ultimate level of freedom from our wounds. If it is in your ability to do so, bless the one who has hurt you. Some examples are sending a holiday card, writing a letter, sending a text, or having a loving phone call. Be a good child to the best of your ability. Even if the person never reaches the ability to be a great parent, honor that person with mercy and bless him or her from time to time. In some cases of abuse, this may not be possible, and that is understandable. Also, some parents may have passed away. In these cases, consider writing a letter and throwing it away or visiting their graves with a flower and a verbal "I forgive you and I honor you with mercy." God can heal these wounds even after someone has passed away or who is unreachable physically.

5. God's love.

Once you truly forgive your parents or extend mercy to them, your heart will be open for God's love. Take time to listen to Christian music that brings in God's presence and just imagine God as your father and rest in his love. He is our God and father, and his Spirit and his love is in us all. Let his love and his presence flow through you today and heal that parent wound. "One God and Father of all, who is above all, and through all, and in you all" (Ephesians 4:6, KJV).

Reflection Journal

Is there a family wound that affected you in the past? If yes, explain. Write a detailed paper for each of the offenses to begin the process for forgiveness. Writing it in detail brings the pain to the top so it can be healed. Many of us have several people and wounds from our pasts. If so, get a notebook specially for this.

_____

_____

_____

_____

_____

List at least one way you could bless or honor this person to truly bring healing and freedom.

_____

_____

_____

_____

_____

"Bless them that curse you and pray for them which despitefully use you" (Luke 6:28, KJV).

If you know you need to forgive a parent but when you think of or are around him or her you're still upset, offended, or angry, you must fast. The Bible says some things only come out by prayer and fasting. Some cuts are so deep that you must fast to get that true freedom from them.

"However, this kind does not go out except by prayer and fasting" (Mathew 17:21, NKJV).

DAY 18

BEING AN OVERCOMER

To be an overcomer is to succeed at dealing with a problem or to master or beat something coming against you. The opposite is to go down, give up, fall, or give up. There are a few keys to being an overcomer. The enemy's job is to bring you fear, discouragement, distraction, and defeat. Our emotions are easily convinced that a situation is hopeless, and then we give up. Let me teach you a pattern and what the word of God says about being an overcomer.

Healing

1.Bring it to God.
In God, we have peace when we bring each struggle, hardship, or situation to him. He gives peace, harmony, and order to our stress, worry, and discouragement. Go to him for his peace and rest in any situation. "Peace I leave with you, my peace I give unto you: not as the world giveth, give I unto you. Let not your heart be troubled, neither let it be afraid" (John 14:27, KJV).

"Come unto me, all ye that labour and are heavy laden, and I will give you rest" (Matthew 11:28, KJV).

2.Don't be surprised by life's issues.
God tells us we will have tribulations and struggles. If we keep in mind that everyone is going to have trouble, we will not be so overwhelmed when it happens. "Beloved, think it not strange concerning the fiery trial which is to try you, as though some strange thing happened unto

you: but rejoice to the extent that you partake of Christ's sufferings, that when His glory is revealed, you may also be glad with exceeding joy" (1 Peter 4:12–13, NKJV).

3.Be encouraged.

The word tells us to take courage. Everything we go through is no surprise to God. We have to remember that and keep ourselves encouraged. David encouraged himself in the Lord, and we must do the same. Remind yourself of how God brought you through your trials last time and have faith he will do it again. Often, we testify to ourselves and to others of all he has and will do again. *Fear not* is written in the Bible 365 times, one for each day of the year.

Lord, help us to keep our courage up and fear under our fear. When the enemy says to give in or give up, we must hold on and press forward. We are overcomers!

"And David was greatly distressed; for the people spake of stoning him, because the soul of all the people was grieved, every man for his sons and for his daughters: but David encouraged himself in the LORD his God" (1 Samuel 30:6, KJV).

"And they overcame him by the blood of the Lamb, and by the word of their testimony" (Revelation 12:11, KJV).

Reflection Journal

What are a few things in your life that you should refuse to give up on?

_____

_____

_____

_____

_____

What can you do today to begin to overcome, conquer, master, or beat this situation?

_____

_____

_____

_____

_____

DAY 19

GRIEF OR DEATH

Grief can be caused by losing someone or something to death or by the loss of a thing or a relationship. My husband, Mark, had his brother die in his arms of a heart attack. I had a child turn eighteen, and by nineteen never speak to me again (one day she will). I have seen firsthand how grief or death can take us to a place that some never find their way back from. Certain things hit us so hard that we feel like our hearts have literally melted. At times, the heaviness makes our hearts feel like they actually sank down from our chests. We are not the only ones who have experienced this. Asaph and Solomon wrote scriptures about grief.

"My flesh and my heart fail; But God is the strength of my heart and my portion forever" (Psalm [of Asaph] 73:26, KJV).

"Heaviness in the heart of man maketh it stoop: but a good word maketh it glad" (Proverb [of Solomon] 12:25, KJV).

Healing
1. Trust God.
"Commit thy way unto the LORD; trust also in him; and he shall bring it to pass" (Psalm 37:5, KJV).

"The righteous perisheth, and no man layeth it to heart: and merciful men are taken away, none considering that the righteous is taken away from the evil to come" (Isaiah 57:1, KJV).

If it's a death, we must realize that God may have saved the person from something worse—even if we didn't think the person was ready to go. God may have allowed him or her time to make some things right in their final moments that we know nothing about. We serve a merciful God. If we lost someone in a relationship, a job, an opportunity, or a plan failed, there is hope. As Psalm 37:5 said, we can give it to God and trust him to bring it back if it was for us, and if it wasn't, we can trust him to bless us with something else.

2. Never lose your faith.
We must remember that God is a good father and must keep our faith even in the hard times. When we really believe in God, then we believe his word is true. His word says that all things work together for good, even when they don't feel good. We can also believe that if it was not the will of God, then he can heal all things and is busy rerouting the situation and turning it around to make it good.

"And we know that all things work together for good to them that love God, to them who are the called according to his purpose" (Romans 8:28, KJV).

"So, Joseph died, being a hundred and ten years old: and they embalmed him, and he was put in a coffin in Egypt" (Genesis 50:26, KJV).

This is the only place in the original text of scripture that the word *coffin* is used. In the study of Greek, the definition for this word was "chest." A hope chest is where you store something for later. When someone dies in the Lord, they are not gone, my friend; but they are put up for later.

Reflection Journal

List two things you lost that have grieved you deeply.

_____

_____

Have you lost someone to death in the past whose grief you need to heal from?

_____

_____

_____

_____

_____

DAY 20

VISION

What is the vision for your life? What is next? I honestly was not aware that I needed a vision. The word of God actually says that without a vision, God's people perish or die. If we are not moving forward or having something to look forward to spiritually, we go backward and sometimes lose our walk with God. Many call this backsliding.

Healing
"Where there is no vision, the people perish" (Proverb 29:18, KJV).

I was once told that if you don't have a vision for yourself and a vision for your family, you will go backward. These are the steps that God showed me to use so that never happens. Follow these four steps to keep a vision in your life and for your family or ministry.

1. Make a list.
Make a list of the things you have thought of or even been told that could be a possibility for you, your family, or ministry. These can be small or big visions.

Then the LORD answered me and said: "Write the vision and make it plain on tablets, that he may run who reads it." (Habakkuk 2:2, NKJV).

2. Seek God's counsel.
Ask God to show you if this is his idea or yours. When we ask God to give us a sign about if something is his will, he answers. He may show you a billboard with a word on it, send a CD, or have someone speak it

over you. Look and listen for his reply. "First seek the counsel of God" (1 Kings 22:5, KJV).

3. Seek personal counsel.
Seek personal counsel from your pastor or mentor. Be sure this person is someone who has had godly success in his or her spiritual life. Be careful who you allow to speak into your life. Only get counsel from someone you trust with your ideas, dreams, and visions.

4. Wait on God.
We all struggle with slowing down and waiting on the reply from God. I like to call waiting a Christian curse word. No one wants to hear it, and no one really wants to do it. When we wait on God, he makes it easier, blessed, stronger, and he does it right.

"Wait on the LORD; Be of good courage, And He shall strengthen your heart; Wait, I say, on the LORD!" (Psalm 27:14, NKJV).

Reflection Journal

List some ideas, dreams, and visions you have for the future.

_____

_____

_____

_____

_____

Pray and ask God if any of these are in his will.

_____

_____

_____

_____

_____

Who can you go to for godly counsel? List three names.

_____

_____

_____

_____

If we don't run ahead of God, he will strengthen us for the journey and bless our paths.

FEAR AND ANXIETY

Each person has experienced fear and anxiety. It is inevitable that we will encounter these emotions. It's what we do with them that makes or breaks us. Fear and anxiety can be described as feeling nervous or distressed, having mental and emotional uncertainty, or feeling panicky. One of the biggest things I have learned is that fear is a bully. Hunters are not allowed to hunt deer at night with a spotlight. The reason it is not legal is because it makes the sport unfair for the deer. When the light hits a deer in the eyes, it becomes paralyzed with fear, unable to think or run away. Fear and anxiety often do the same thing to us when we are presented with questions like, "How long will this take? What's going to happen? Do they think bad of me?" and more. The trick of the enemy is that this causes us to be left like the deer—fruitless, without direction, unable to move forward, and without confidence or courage.

Healing

"Fear not, for I am with you; be not dismayed, for I am your God. I will strengthen you, yes, I will help you, I will uphold you with My righteous right hand" (Isaiah 41:10, NJKV).

In this verse, God gives us five mighty things that he will do for us. Let us make no mistake: our God is strong, and he is able to do all things. He simply asks us not to do two things. First, do not fear getting frozen by Satan's trap of what-ifs. And second, do not be dismayed by forgetting who you are and what you're doing. A boxer gets dismayed when he is hit so hard that he stumbles, usually forgetting at the moment who he is and what he is doing. If we don't lose our vision and instead get caught in God's promises to be with us, to be our God, to strengthen us, to help us, and to uphold us with his right hand (powerful hand), we will know he is able.

Be strong and of good courage, do not fear nor be afraid of them; for the LORD your God, He is the One who goes with you. He will not leave you nor forsake you" (Deuteronomy 31:6, NKJV).

Some of us had a big brother to go with us in times of trouble as youths. But even if not, we all have the God of heaven saying, "I will go with you, and I will not leave you, forsake you, or abandon you." There have even been times when I got myself into the situation at hand, and God still stood by me. He will stand by you too. In my hardest moments, I heard a whisper, "Be strong and have courage." He is the lion of the tribe of Judah, and he walks with us. One translation even says that he goes before us. Amen.

"Trust in the LORD with all thine heart; and lean not unto thine own understanding" (Proverb 3:5, KJV).

Remember that trust is the opposite of fear. Fear is not knowing and being nervous. Trust is not knowing and still having faith in God.

Reflection Journal

What situations have the enemy used in the last few years to cause you to be paralyzed with fear?

_____

_____

_____

_____

_____

List three things in this season that you need to begin trusting God with and turn from fear.

_____

_____

_____

What have you trusted God for in the past?

_____

_____

_____

_____

DAY 22

WHEN PROTECTION FEELS LIKE REJECTION

Have you ever wanted something so badly and, at the last minute you lost it, it left, or God said no, that you can't have it? This is an opportunity for growth or failure. In these moments, you will be so tempted to give up. At times, we play with the idea that this thing would be worth all that would be lost. It's normal to go back and forth in faith and in knowing that God has reasons for saying no, but then also feeling like you can never have anything you want—with a side of depression. If or when this happens to you, follow these steps to freedom.

Healing
1. Give it to God.
Give all the broken pieces of your heart, all the time, hope, and effort that you wasted on this thing or person, give it to God. This requires trust that God is good and would not ask us to give it up if it would be good for us. Sometimes we can't see why God said no or wait and later we will understand, if we trust him. "For we walk by faith, not by sight" (2 Corinthians 5:7, KJV).

2. Allow yourself to grieve.
Allow yourself time to grieve who or what you lost. This may look like three days of Netflix, several days of going only from the bed to the sofa, or saying, "Lord, I understand one minute and am on

the floor crying and kicking the next." Either way, pain demands to be felt. A short season of feeling our losses is very normal. And God hears our cries and is near us to comfort us. He knows it breaks our hearts to lose certain people or things, even if they were not good for us.

"The righteous cry, and the LORD heareth, and delivereth them out of all their troubles.
The LORD is near to those who have a broken heart" (Psalm 34:17–18, KJV).

3. Acceptance.
Find some way to accept what happened and why that thing didn't work out. Accept why it wasn't good for you and what would've happened if things had worked out the way you'd planned after all. Again, sometimes we just have to trust that God can see over the hill we are trying to climb.

4. Moving forward.
Pick yourself up, gather all your might, and tell the Lord that you commit your life to his will above your own. Get out of the house, go shopping, or even take walks at the park. Open the door and move forward toward what God has next for you in your life. You will know it's time to move forward when you wake up and feel a nudge to move on. At that point, you have to choose not to stay sad and possibly enter depression. Not moving forward can be dangerous. It can allow a spirit of grief to oppress us and a heaviness to sit on us.

"Commit thy way unto the LORD; trust also in him; and he shall bring it to pass" (Psalm 37:5, KJV).

Reflection Journal

List three things in your past that have felt like rejection but were possibly God protecting you by taking them away.

_____

_____

_____

What negative thing(s) may have happened if those hadn't been removed from your life?

_____

_____

_____

_____

Remember that sometimes, God says no, and sometimes, he says not right now. Lord, help us to trust your will and your timing. "Saying 'Father, if it is Your will, take this cup away from me; nevertheless not my will, but Yours, be done'" (Luke 22:42, NKJV).

DAY 23

ABANDONMENT

Abandonment can come in many forms. Here are some of the most common ways we experience it: Many of us have been left as a child, divorced, cast aside by our children, lost a loved one, or even cast out of a place or a family. The wounds of abandonment can be very deep.

Healing
"When my father and my mother forsake me, then the LORD will take me up" (Psalm 27:10, KJV).

God literally says that when our parents forsake us, he will take us up or move us closer to him. The more abandoned, by the ones who were supposed to love us, the closer the Lord Will draw us to him, if we will allow him too. This isn't just for parents. God will pick you up and hold you closer in any season someone or something casts you aside. Lord, help us to allow you to hold us in those seasons.

"For the LORD will not cast off his people, neither will he forsake his inheritance" (Psalm 94:14, KJV).

"The LORD will not reject his people; he will not abandon his special possession" (Psalm 94:14, NLT).

The Lord will not cast off his people. We are special to him. Many times, we mess up big time and he forgives us. He calls us an inheritance or his special possession. Remember, even if others didn't see your worth, God does. If they don't see your potential, then he will send the ones who will.

"And let us not be weary in well doing for in due season we shall reap, if we faint not" (Galatians 6:9, KJV).

Abandonment cuts to the soul. If we allow it to, it can become a spiritually—and sometimes physically—fatal wound. Years afterward, the memories and pain of abandonment can creep in and try to sit on us again. Don't allow the times you were abandoned in the past cause you to forfeit your future. If we allow it to, it can cause us to live in insecurity, to build walls, to run away, to become angry and prideful, or to live in self-pity, jealousy, and bitterness, dwelling in depression or becoming a people pleaser, backsliding, or even considering suicide. The word of God promises that blessings are coming later if we do not give up or faint in these near-fatal seasons.

Reflection Journal

What are the deepest memories you have of experiencing abandonment or being cast aside?

_____

_____

_____

_____

_____

What negative ways were you tempted with to deal with those situations?

_____

_____

_____

_____

_____

What scriptures or songs help you overcome these feelings when they creep up?

_____

_____

_____

_____

_____

Each time the enemy comes back around to bring those old feelings of abandonment, resist him. Never forget that you're not that little girl, boy, abused spouse, or tormented person anymore. You are who God says you are. You are wanted.

"Submit yourselves therefore to God. Resist the devil, and he will flee from you" (James 4:7, KJV).

When you struggle with feeling abandoned, listen to the song "Wanted" by Dara Maclean and "You Say" by Lauren Daigle.

DAY 24

BITTERNESS AND OFFENSES

The dictionary calls bitterness feelings of anger, hurt, or resentment from unjust treatment. I think of the temptation of bitterness like a fish swallowing a hook. Things that happen to us offer a temptation to swallow it. If we do this becomes bitterness in our belly and it will poison our entire life. I have found by trial and error in my own life that there is a process to overcome bitterness and I will share it with you. The Bible is clear that every person will have the temptation of bitterness and being offended.

Healing
1.Don't be surprised.
When someone offends you, do not allow it to surprise you. Remind yourself that hardship and offenses will come to everyone.

Then he said to the disciples, "It is impossible that no offenses should come, but woe to him through whom they do come!" (Luke 17:1, NKJV).

Remember, the word of God said it is impossible for us never to be hurt, mistreated, or offended. This is part of life.

2. Admit it.
Often, it feels better to stuff down or deny an offense, but we get so much relief when we dig it up. If swallowing it is the bait, then digging it up is freedom. The easiest way to dig up the offense, along with its roots of bitterness, is to write it down. Write in detail about what was said or

done to you or your family member(s). This causes all of the emotions surrounding the situation to rise up so you can really deal with them.

3. Forgive them.

Forgiveness is an act of your will at first. It doesn't always come with fuzzy feelings. At the bottom of the page where you have written about the offense and bitterness in detail, write a forgiveness scripture reminding yourself why you forgive. For example: "But if ye forgive not men their trespasses, neither will your father forgive your trespasses" (Matthew 6:15, KJV).

4. Fast.

If you were deeply hurt, wounded, or offended by something and a root of bitterness has begun to grow or has been there a long time, like a hook in your belly, you will have to fast to get it out. As I mentioned previously, fasting is going a certain amount of time without certain foods or drinks while giving yourself to prayer. Ask God during this fast to help you let this thing go. And on the last day of your fast, do these steps over.

"However, this kind does not go out except by prayer and fasting" (Matthew 17:21, NKJV).

5. Bless and pray for them.

In some little or big way, bless the one who has previously hurt you. Even if the blessing is just speaking to him or her again, sending a kind card or letter, or something bigger like taking the person to lunch or sending him or her a gift card. Add the person to your daily prayer list and genuinely pray for God to do something good for him or her. When you obey God's Word and bless and pray for those who have hurt you, the amount of freedom you will experience will take your breath away. Your hatred and animosity will fly out the window.

"But I say unto you, love your enemies, bless them that curse you, do good to them that hate you, and pray for them which despitefully use you, and persecute you" (Matthew 5:44, KJV).

Reflection Journal

Who has been or what has happened in your past that causes you to become bitter?

_____

_____

_____

_____

_____

Are you still hurt and bitter about this situation? If so, will you try these steps to true freedom?

_____

_____

_____

_____

_____

Jesus knows how hard it can be to forgive the ones who hurt us the deepest, but he doesn't ask us to do something he didn't do himself.

Then Jesus said, "Father, forgive them, for they do not know what they do. And they divided His garments and cast lots" (Luke 23:34, NKJV).

DAY 25

SCARS

The scars that lie on our hearts cannot be seen like the ones that are on the outside. Even though they cannot be seen, they can very much be felt. Emotional scars can be defined by a lasting effect from grief, fear, or any other emotion left on a person's heart. These scars often come from a traumatic experience and can deeply change our character. We will look at some of these scars and the healing and comfort that God leaves for us.

Healing
"Now may our Lord Jesus Christ Himself, and our God and Father, who has loved us and given us everlasting consolation and good hope by grace, comfort your hearts, and establish you in every good word and work" (2 Thessalonians 2:16–17, KJV).

Emotional scars can come from death, divorce, loss, abuse, and many other places. No one is exempt from trauma. It seems like at the least expecting time, it enters our lives, and no one is ever fully prepared.

The Devil's Plan
The devil look for ways to destroy and torment us and our families in our weakest moments. When pain, death, trauma, and scars enter our lives, his plan is for us to use drugs, lust, have shame or depression, or even attempt suicide to escape.

"The thief cometh not, but for to steal, and to kill, and to destroy ..." (John 10:10, KJV).

God's Plan

God calls us out of the sin and shame that we buried our pain in. He has a plan for us and can make a purpose from it. "Awake to righteousness, and do not sin; for some do not have the knowledge of God. I say this to your shame" (1 Corinthians 15:34, KJV).

He speaks his word of healing to our shame and self-hatred, and he calls us to arise in his ways and in his knowledge. He awakens us to turn our hearts to his right ways.

"Unless the LORD had been my help, my soul had almost dwelt in silence. When I said, my foot slippeth; thy mercy, O LORD, held me up" (Psalm 94:18, NKJV).

He has our backs, even when we cause pain. We all know there are times when we get scars that are no fault of our own. Then there are times when we had a lot to do with our own hurts. We serve a God who will help us even when we mess up.

"Then I went down to the potter's house, and there he was, making something at the wheel, And the vessel that he made of clay was marred in the hand of the potter; so he made it again into another vessel, as it seemed good to the potter to make" (Jeremiah 18:3–4, NKJV).

"Come, and let us return to the LORD; For He has torn, but He will heal us; He has stricken, but He will bind us up" (Hosea 6:1, KJV).

Reflection Journal

What scars have traumatic things left on your heart?

_____

_____

_____

_____

_____

Are you ready to put your heart in God's hands and allow him to turn your pain into a purpose? In what way could God possibly use your pain to help others?

_____

_____

_____

_____

_____

Any way you think God could use your pain for a purpose is a blessing. The enemy will make you feel ignorant for even making an effort. Don't allow him to steal your blessing. Step out and help someone else with what you have been through.

ADDICTION AND LUST

Addiction is something in this generation that almost every family has been touched by. In the beginning, using a substance is fun, or it covers a pain we think we can no longer carry. Then comes the moment we realize we cannot stop. Addictions are usually to drugs, alcohol, or perceptions.

Lust is very similar. It often feels good in the beginning. Unfortunately, after a while, we seem to need it and even crave it. It can be unmarried sex, porn, adultery, or even being addicted to attention obtained by dressing or acting seductive.

Healing
It takes wisdom to overcome these things. Rehab will teach us that insanity is doing the same thing over and over and expecting a different result. Wisdom is looking at how addictions trap you and learning how not to fall into the same pit again.

"Wisdom is the principal thing; therefore, get wisdom: and with all thy getting get understanding" (Proverb 4:7, KJV).

1. Admit.
Look at what happened and admit your fault in it. The Bible calls this repenting. Once we humble ourselves to admit that we have an issue, God can work with that. Even when, at first, we are able to admit it only to him. I was once told the only thing God can't change is what

we will not admit. This changed my life. I now know that if we don't admit our faults (at least to God), we can never be set free from them.

2. Break agreement and relationship with it.
Break up with it. Sometimes we literally need to say out loud that we break up with something and then act on it. Get rid of the computer, change your number, get off the internet, burn the prescriptions, and end the ungodly relationships.

"Be ye not unequally yoked together with unbelievers: for what fellowship hath righteousness with unrighteousness? and what communion hath light with darkness?" (2 Corinthians 6:14, KJV).

3. Fast.
When you have a true addiction, it will require you to humble yourself and your desires. We have spoiled ourselves by giving into any and every desire we have. To get self-control back, we can fast. To deny the flesh gives your spirit the strength to say no.

"However, this kind does not go out except by prayer and fasting" (Matthew 17:21, NKJV).

Reflection Journal

Have you struggled with addictions or lust in your past? If so, explain.

_____

_____

_____

_____

_____

What helped you, in the past, to overcome these issues?

_____

_____

_____

_____

_____

What are you struggling with now?

_____

_____

_____

_____

_____

DAY 27

CUTTING AND SELF-HARM

In the last several years, cutting and self-harm have become a big thing. When you ask someone why he or she tried it, you may get answers like, "To let me pain out" or "The physical pain takes away the mental pain for a little while." I will not say that it doesn't feel like a temporary relief because I have not tried it. God showed me in his word that it is against his will and that it allows a tormenting spirit to attach itself to our lives. Let's take a look.

Did you know that not cutting yourself is found in the Bible?

"You are the children of the LORD your God; you shall not cut yourselves nor shave the front of your head for the dead. For you are a holy people to the LORD your God, and the LORD has chosen you to be a people for Himself, a special treasure above all the peoples who are on the face of the earth" (Deuteronomy 14:1–2, NKJV).

A spirit of torment is attached to cutting, self-hatred, deep depression, and excessive grief from the past. Mark 5:1–9 (NKJV) says this:

> Then they came to the other side of the sea, to the country of the Gadarenes. And when He had come out of the boat, immediately there met Him out of the tombs a man with an unclean spirit, who had his dwelling among the tombs; and no one could bind him, not even with chains, because he had often been bound with shackles and chains. And the chains had been

pulled apart by him, and the shackles broken in pieces; neither could anyone tame him. And always, night and day, he was in the mountains and in the tombs, crying out and cutting himself with stones. When he saw Jesus from afar, he ran and worshiped Him. And he cried out with a loud voice and said, "What have I to do with You, Jesus, Son of the Most High God? I implore You by God that You do not torment me." For He said to him, "Come out of the man, unclean spirit!" Then He asked him, "What is your name?" And he answered, saying, "My name is Legion; for we are many."

This man stayed in the tombs day and night, cutting himself. Why do you think he was is the graveyard? Could it be because he wouldn't let things go from his past and they tormented his mind? Could it be that when he gave into the temptation of cutting and self-harm, he gave permission for a very bad demon to torment him? God doesn't tell us not to cut ourselves for no reason. You may hear the lies that promise you peace if you cut yourself or harm yourself, but just like the man in the Bible, it did not bring peace.

Healing
1. Repent.
Ask God to forgive us, and he will both forgive and cleanse us. "If we confess our sins, He is faithful and just to forgive us our sins and to cleanse us from all unrighteousness" (1 John 1:9, KJV).

2. Run to Jesus.
Just like the man in Mark 5 we can run to Jesus in prayer, at an altar, in a prayer line, or beside your bed, and he will set us free with his mighty power!

"Now the Lord is that Spirit: and where the Spirit of the Lord is, there is liberty" (2 Corinthians 3:17, KJV).

Reflection Journal

Have you cut yourself in the past?

_____

_____

_____

_____

_____

If so, are you willing to try these steps to be set free?

_____

_____

_____

_____

_____

DAY 28

THE MIND

The mind is the part of a person that allows him or her to think, feel, and understand. We all win or lose battles because of the way we think. The way you think about things is the position you take. It's the side you choose to be on. What side you agree with is the side that you are on.

Healing
"As a man thinks in his heart, so is he" (Proverb 23:7, KJV).

When you are thinking about something today, tomorrow, you will be acting on it. Imagine that your thoughts are your steps as you walk toward something. Within the next day, week, or year, you will be standing in the middle of what you were once only thinking about.

"Then when lust (the desires thought of) has conceived, it bringeth forth: and sin, when it is finished, bringeth forth death" (James 1:15, KJV).

Follow these three steps that help us get victory in our mind and in our lives:

1. Examine.
When we examine our thoughts, we can find out what we battle with the most so it's not able to sneak up on us as easily.

2. Break agreement.
If you come to agreement with something in your thoughts, or if you agree with something bad and think about it often, you give it

permission to get increasingly stronger in your life. Then, you become its slave. If we realize what we are thinking about and break up with it, it loses all power in our lives. We can say, "I do not agree with that or want to think of or do it. I rebuke those thoughts, repent for thinking about them, and God, I ask you to deliver me from the enemy that's sending me these thoughts as a trap because this is not how I feel. In Jesus's name."

"Don't you realize that you become the slave of whatever you choose to obey? You can be a slave to sin, which leads to death, or you can choose to obey God, which leads to righteous living" (Romans 6:16, NLT).

3. Think on good things.
Think about positive things on purpose to replace the lies. Look up scripture that shares the way God feels about how the enemy was trying to get you to think about these subjects.

"Finally, brethren, whatever things are true, whatever things are noble, whatever things are just, whatever things are pure, whatever things are lovely, whatever things are of good report, if there is any virtue and if there is anything praiseworthy—meditate on these things" (Philippians 4:8, NKJV).

Reflection Journal

Have you battled thinking about bad or harmful things in the past? If so, what were they?

_____

_____

_____

_____

_____

Will you break agreement with them and admit that they're not good or true, and that you don't want bad things in your life ?

_____

_____

_____

_____

_____

Write three scriptures about the subjects that share the truth about the lies the enemy was trying to get you to believe. If you don't know any scriptures, you can look them up on your phone or by looking up those keywords in the glossary in the back of your Bible. This is called studying the word.

_____

_____

_____

DAY 29

RETURN TO HOPE

Hope is a feeling of expectation or a strong desire for something. Several years ago, the Lord showed me that we would open an addiction refuge. A few years passed, and I felt the Lord was showing me it was about to happen. The next month, the entire world shut down with the coronavirus pandemic. I was disappointed. Then some of the very people I was trying to help slandered and blasted me in private, to others, and on social media. I was driving down the road and I heard, "What's the point? Give up and get even with them." I honestly felt like doing all three. I went to God and asked, "What is going on, Lord?" He showed me how Paul was sent to save the gentiles, but he was put on trial and judged wrongly by the very ones he was sent to save. Last, God showed me that his hope and love was put on trial. This happens to many of us. If we want to accomplish our purposes and win the battles, it's not by getting even. To win the battle, we must keep hope when it is hopeless and love others when they are persecuting us. We win when we continue to love them and continue to hope when it looks hopeless.

Healing
"For this cause, I, Paul, the prisoner of Jesus Christ for you Gentiles" (Ephesians 3:1, KJV).

Paul's cause was to bring Jesus to the people, and they arrested him. He went willingly, even though jail was the main platform he would preach from. But when Paul perceived that one part was Sadducees and the other Pharisees, he cried out in the council, "Men and brethren, I am a Pharisee, the son of a Pharisee; concerning the hope and resurrection of the dead I am being judged!" (Acts 23:6, NKJV).

For his hope and his purpose, he was on trial and being judged. But Paul held on to his hope. "And because lawlessness will abound, the love of many will grow cold" (Matthew 24:12, NKJV).

Paul did not lose his love even through all the hurt and persecution. "Verily, verily, I say unto you, except a corn of wheat fall into the ground and die, it abideth alone: but if it die, it bringeth forth much fruit" (John 12:24, KJV).

Some seasons feel like death. Through the pain, we produce the ability to help many and not just help ourselves.

"Return to the stronghold, You prisoners of hope. Even today I declare that I will rest" (Zechariah 9:12, NKJV).

Return to your stronghold. A stronghold is a position in war. We are prisoners of hope. We will still hope when we can't see a reason to anymore. Even if years pass and it looks like we are going backward, we will hold our positions of hope.

Reflection Journal

Have you given up on something, someone, abandoned hope, or allowed your love to grow cold?

_____

_____

_____

_____

_____

If you have, then remembered the things that God told you he would do or that he would do through you and write them down. Remind yourself of these promises. Write the vision when you are discouraged, and then write it again.

_____

_____

_____

_____

_____

"Then the LORD answered me and said: 'Write the vision and make it plain on tablets, That he may run who reads it. For the vision is yet for an appointed time; But at the end it will speak, and it will not lie. Though it tarries, wait for it; Because it will surely come, It will not tarry'" (Habakkuk 2:2–3, NKJV).

Remember:
The Valley of Achor is a statement from the story in the book of Joshua, where Achan sinned and an entire group of people paid for his sin of disobedience. Later, because of his sin, his entire family was killed. This last scripture is a promise that your biggest mistake, your longest battle, or your bloodiest battle can later be made into a door of hope. The very thing that brought pain and devastation will now be a place of praise, healing, and hope for others. Come out of that thing as when they came out of Egypt and come home to the promised land. The Lord will use this battle to save others.

"I will give her vineyards from there, and the Valley of Achor as a door of hope; She shall sing there, As in the days of her youth, As in the day when she came up from the land of Egypt" (Hosea 2:15, NKJV).

What situation in your life do you need to come back to, come out of, or begin to use that bloody battle—the one that almost killed you—as a door of hope to many?

_____

_____

_____

_____

_____

DAY 30

WISDOM

Wisdom is to have experience, knowledge, and good judgment. If we have good judgment, it is usually because we have learned what not to do from our failures. Failures try to give us shame, but if we look at them and learn from them, they are what produces true and lifelong wisdom. I've often heard my pastor, Jerry Terrell, say, "You learn the most in life through your biggest failures." It is our decision if we use our failures as shame or as wisdom to fuel our futures.

Healing

"The thief does not come except to steal, and to kill, and to destroy. I have come that they may have life, and that they may have it more abundantly" (John 10:10, NKJV).

"Lest Satan should take advantage of us; for we are not ignorant of his devices" (2 Corinthians 2:11, NKJV).

The word of God says we are not ignorant of the ways the enemy tries to take us out, defeat, and destroy us. If we will take the time to look back at our past failures, then we will learn wisdom from them instead of being defeated by them. The enemy's nature is to steal, kill, and destroy. God instructed me many years ago to make a list of things the enemy used to try to steal, kill and destroy my life.

My Wisdom List

1. Addiction.

I was a drug addict, homeless, and hopeless for five years of my life. I went from a few pills and beers to crack cocaine, meth, and prostitution. I called out to God while lying on the floor of a crack house, and his spirit came to me and he led me out. Each chapter I've written is something that he walked me through. Every time I have success, the enemy is there to offer me back to addiction through a pill, a beer, a diet pill, or any other form he can sneak under the radar, attempting to trap me. I even watch my intake of energy drinks. I don't want to allow anything an opportunity to sneak back in. Addiction is the number-one way the enemy tries to bring me backward.

2. Lust/bad relationship.

Premarital sex, pornography, adultery, or forbidden relationships, even homosexuality fall into this category. I committed adultery and destroyed my first marriage. Lust is something the enemy brings my way often to tempt me. He may show me someone good looking or whisper suggestions in my ears. God showed me long ago that when I opened the door of adultery in my first marriage, addiction, lies, and divorce came in also. So, I know that no matter what rough patch my marriage goes through, adultery is a doorway for many enemies to enter and destroy all that God has given me. So, yes, I can see when someone is good looking, but I remind myself that no matter how good looking that person is, it's not worth losing my family and blessings. Besides, after six months, any human will get on my nerves. I also remind myself that that person wouldn't bless me in the way my husband does, and I gladly walk right on by.

3. Condemnation.

The first two list items were things that came at me from the outside. Condemnation is a voice on the inside that whispers, "You're not good enough; you can't make it; everyone knows who you used to be," and the list goes on. These voices were one of the reasons I ended up in adultery and addiction. I didn't know how to shut them up. So, I laid on the sofa for six months in depression. The enemy always tries to bring this back around. Now, when I realize this voice is whispering lies to me, I turn on loud Christian music and read the scriptures that tell me he is merciful, doesn't condemn me, loves me, and forgives me. (See the following scriptures: Psalm 103:14, KJV; 1 John 3:20, KJV; and 1 John 1:9, KJV.)

4. Discouragement.

Discouragement is when I lose my desire to serve God, to be sober, to go to class, or to read my word. Some may call this a dry season or being fainthearted and ready to give up. This happens to me at least once a year, and I remind myself that this even happens to the men in the Bible (Job 23:10, KJV). Job couldn't feel God, but he said he knew the path he took. He kept going even when he didn't feel like it. If you keep doing what you know to do, this will pass for you also. I always talk to someone who is positive, write a list of the things that God has done for me in the past, and I keep doing what I know to do. And as quick as it started, it will end.

In 1 Samuel 30:6 (KJV), David encouraged himself in the Lord.

5. Division.

Dividing from a church in my first marriage was the first thing that happened to us. This was step one before the condemnation that led to depression and before the adultery and addiction. The very first thing that happened was we were divided from our church and church family over a misunderstanding, and my feelings were hurt. At least once a year, the enemy tries to get me to divide from the people or the places God has planted me. I pray for the ones I feel anger toward. Then I ask God for his perfect will. Last, I fast for God to show me the truth, and I do not move until he shows me. There have been very few times when God ever says to leave. Indeed, he has told me to leave a place since then, but only once in the last twelve years. When he puts us somewhere, it's for a purpose.

Reflection Journal

Can you relate to some of the ways I mentioned that the enemy tries to take me out? List the ones that come against you too.

_____

_____

_____

_____

Look at your life and write down a list of things that have ruined your life or have set you back. List the ways the enemy comes against you often.

_____

_____

_____

_____

Printed in the United States
by Baker & Taylor Publisher Services